PET-SIZED DINOS

by Natalie Lunis

Consultant: Luis M. Chiappe, Ph.D.
Director of the Dinosaur Institute
Natural History Museum of Los Angeles County

BEARPORT
PUBLISHING

NEW YORK, NEW YORK

Credits

Title Page, © Luis Rey; TOC, © Julius Csotonyi; 4, © Luis Rey; 5, © Luis Rey; 6, © John Sibbick; 7, © Spencer Platt/Getty Images; 8, © DEA PICTURE LIBRARY/Getty Images; 9, © De Agostini Picture Library/The Natural History Museum, London; 10, © De Agostini Picture Library/The Natural History Museum, London; 11, © De Agostini Picture Library/The Natural History Museum, London; 12, © Luis Rey; 13, © Publiphoto/Photo Researchers, Inc.; 14, T02319 Triceratops, Upper Cretaceous Period (70-65 million years ago), Snowball, Peter (20th century)/Natural History Museum, London, UK,/The Bridgeman Art Library International; 15, © De Agostini Picture Library/The Natural History Museum, London; 16, © KPA Archival Collection/Omni-Photo Communications, Inc.; 17, © Michael Skrepnick; 18, © Michael Skrepnick; 19, © Julius Csotonyi; 20, © Louie Psihoyos/Corbis; 21, © John Sibbick; 23TL, © De Agostini Picture Library/The Natural History Museum, London; 23TR, © Luis Rey; 23BL, © Spencer Platt/Getty Images; 23BR, © Jozsef Szasz-Fabian/Shutterstock.

Publisher: Kenn Goin
Editorial Director: Adam Siegel
Creative Director: Spencer Brinker
Design: Dawn Beard Creative
Cover Illustration: Luis Rey
Photo Researcher: Omni-Photo Communications, Inc.

Library of Congress Cataloging-in-Publication Data

Lunis, Natalie.
Pet-sized dinos / by Natalie Lunis.
   p. cm. — (Dino times trivia)
Includes bibliographical references and index.
ISBN-13: 978-1-59716-710-9 (library binding)
ISBN-10: 1-59716-710-X (library binding)
1. Dinosaurs—Juvenile literature. 2. Size perception—Juvenile literature. I. Title.

QE861.5.L86 2009
567.9—dc22
                      2008006174

For more information, write to Bearport Publishing Company, Inc., 101 Fifth Avenue, Suite 6R, New York, New York 10003. Printed in the United States of America.

10 9 8 7 6 5 4 3 2 1

Contents

Tiny Dinosaurs

Many different kinds of **dinosaurs** once lived on Earth. Some were huge—as long as three school buses. Others were very small—the size of dogs, cats, and chickens.

In this book, you'll read about eight pet-sized dinosaurs. Don't expect to find them in anyone's home, however. Like all dinosaurs, they disappeared more than 65 million years ago!

So far scientists have found **fossils** of about 800 different kinds of dinosaurs. They are finding more every year.

Microraptor

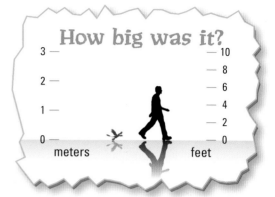
How do you say it?
mye-kroh-RAP-tur

What does it mean?
small thief

Microraptor was one of the smallest dinosaurs that ever lived.

How small was it?

Microraptor was about 2.5 feet (.7 m) long—the size of a crow with a very long tail.

6

Scientists can't be sure which dinosaur was the smallest. Why? The tiniest bones they find often belong to baby dinosaurs. The scientists have to use what they know to then figure out how big the full-grown dinosaurs would be.

Microraptor fossil

7

Saurornithoides

How do you say it?
sor-orn-ih-THOI-deez

What does it mean?
bird-like reptile

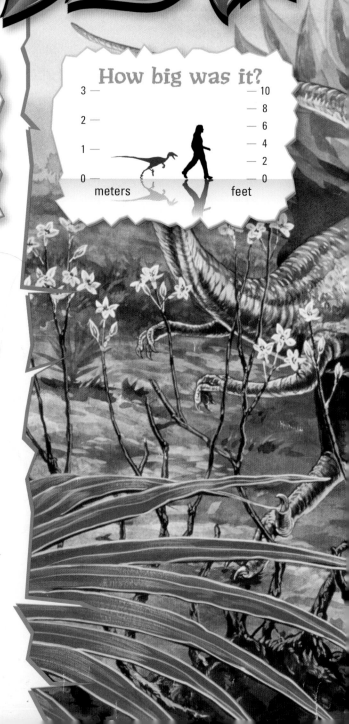

How big was it?

3 — | — 10
2 — | — 8
1 — | — 6
| | — 4
0 — | — 2
| | — 0
meters | feet

Like many pet-sized dinosaurs, *Saurornithoides* was a fast-running hunter.

What animals did it hunt?

Saurornithoides hunted insects, lizards, frogs, and small rat-like **mammals**. It used its hands to grab and hold the small animals that it hunted.

Some small dinosaurs, like *Saurornithoides*, ate only meat. Others ate only plants.

9

Lesothosaurus

How do you say it?
leh-*soh*-thoh-SOR-uhss

What does it mean?
Lesotho reptile
(Lesotho is a country in Africa)

This dog-sized dinosaur had a body that looked like the body of a meat-eater. Yet scientists are almost sure it was a plant-eater.

How do they know?

Scientists can tell that *Lesothosaurus* ate plants by looking at its bony **beak** and pointy teeth. From the way they are shaped, scientists can tell that they were perfect for eating leaves—not meat.

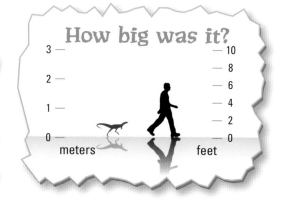

beak

Many kinds of plant-eating dinosaurs had bony beaks. They used them to tear off leaves from plants.

Ornitholestes

How do you say it?
or-*nih*-thoh-LESS-teez

What does it mean?
bird thief

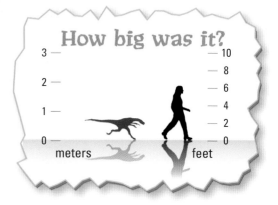
Ornitholestes was a small dinosaur that probably survived by stealing from other dinosaurs.

What did it steal?

Many scientists think that *Ornitholestes* stole and ate the eggs of other dinosaurs.

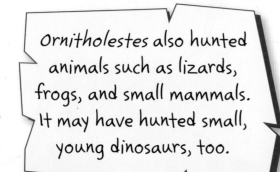

Ornitholestes also hunted animals such as lizards, frogs, and small mammals. It may have hunted small, young dinosaurs, too.

12

Microceratops

How do you say it?
mye-kroh-SER-uh-*tops*

What does it mean?
small-horned face

How big was it?

3 —		— 10
		— 8
2 —		— 6
1 —		— 4
		— 2
0 —		— 0
meters		feet

Microceratops was closely related to a large, well-known dinosaur called *Triceratops*. Like *Triceratops*, it had a large, bony frill sticking up behind its head and covering its neck.

What was the purpose of this frill?

Some scientists think that the frill helped protect the dinosaur during a fight or an attack. Others think that it may have helped hold together the animal's heavy jaws.

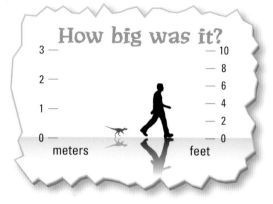

Triceratops frill

14

Microceratops
frill

Microceratops was the size of a small dog. Triceratops was the size of a large elephant.

15

Bambiraptor

How do you say it?
bam-bee-RAP-tur

What does it mean?
thief the size of Bambi

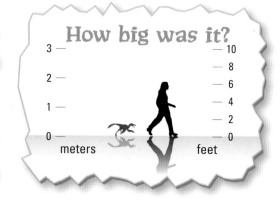

How big was it?

Bambiraptor was a small dinosaur that weighed about as much as a turkey.

How did this small dinosaur get its name?

Wes Linster, a 14-year-old boy, was the first person to find the bones of *Bambiraptor*. The dinosaur's small size made Wes imagine that it was friendly and cute, like the famous animal character Bambi. Scientists later officially named it after this famous deer.

Bambi

In spite of its name, *Bambiraptor* was a fierce meat-eater.

Sinosauropteryx

How do you say it?
sine-oh-sor-OP-tur-iks

What does it mean?
Chinese feathered reptile

How big was it?

meters		feet
3		10
		8
2		6
		4
1		2
0		0

Like many small dinosaurs, *Sinosauropteryx* had fuzzy feathers.

Did the feathers help it fly?

Scientists don't think so. They think the feathers on *Sinosauropteryx* helped keep it warm instead.

fuzzy feathers

Scientists know that *Sinosauropteryx* had feathers because they found remains of them in rocks.

Archaeopteryx

How do you say it?
ar-kee-OP-tur-iks

What does it mean?
ancient wing

How big was it?

3 — — 10
2 — — 8
— — 6
1 — — 4
— — 2
0 — — 0
meters   feet

In 1861, scientists found fossils of a tiny and strange-looking creature. They called it *Archaeopteryx*. It had wings as well as feathers, like today's birds. Yet the animal was also like a dinosaur in many ways.

What important new idea did the discovery of *Archaeopteryx* lead to?

The unusual fossils of *Archaeopteryx* have led many scientists to think that dinosaurs and birds are closely related.

wings

Archaeopteryx fossil

teeth

Many scientists think that Archaeopteryx was the first bird. Unlike today's birds, however, Archaeopteryx had teeth in its beak.

21

Where Did They Live?

This map shows some of the places where the fossils of pet-sized dinosaurs have been found.

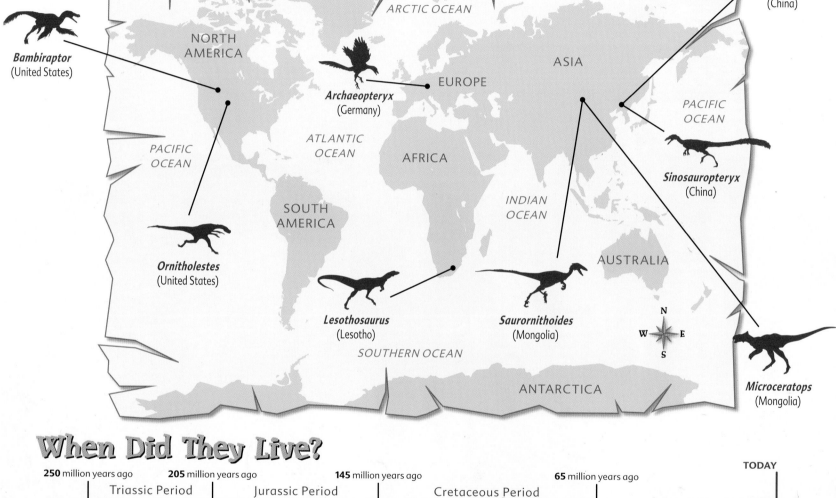

Bambiraptor
(United States)

Archaeopteryx
(Germany)

Microraptor
(China)

ARCTIC OCEAN

NORTH AMERICA

EUROPE

ASIA

PACIFIC OCEAN

PACIFIC OCEAN

ATLANTIC OCEAN

AFRICA

Sinosauropteryx
(China)

Ornitholestes
(United States)

SOUTH AMERICA

INDIAN OCEAN

AUSTRALIA

Lesothosaurus
(Lesotho)

Saurornithoides
(Mongolia)

N
W E
S

SOUTHERN OCEAN

ANTARCTICA

Microceratops
(Mongolia)

When Did They Live?

250 million years ago   **205** million years ago   **145** million years ago   **65** million years ago   **TODAY**

Triassic Period   Jurassic Period   Cretaceous Period

Lesothosaurus

Ornitholestes
Archaeopteryx

Sinosauropteryx
Microraptor

Microceratops
Saurornithoides

Bambiraptor

First dinosaurs appear

Dinosaurs die out

First humans appear

22

Glossary

beak (BEEK)
the hard, pointy part of a dinosaur's mouth used for tearing apart food

dinosaurs
(DYE-nuh-sorz)
reptiles that lived on land more than 65 million years ago, and then died out

fossils
(FOSS-uhlz)
what is left of plants or animals that lived long ago

mammals
(MAM-uhlz)
warm-blooded animals that have a backbone, hair or fur on their skin, and drink their mothers' milk as babies

Index

Read More

Bennett, Leonie. *Amazing Dinosaur Facts.* New York: Bearport Publishing (2008).

Dixon, Dougal. *Scutellosaurus and Other Small Dinosaurs.* Minneapolis, MN: Picture Window Books (2006).

Lessem, Don. *The Smallest Dinosaurs.* Minneapolis, MN: Lerner Publications (2005).

Learn More Online

To learn more about pet-sized dinosaurs, visit
www.bearportpublishing.com/DinoTimesTrivia

About the Author

Natalie Lunis has written more than 30 science and nature books for children. She lives in the New York City area.